Bug-Eyed Loonery

A Play for Young People

Brian L. Bishop

SAMUELFRENCH-LONDON.CO.UK
SAMUELFRENCH.COM

CHARACTERS

Simple Simon
Wee Willie Winkie
Septimus Spider
The Old Woman Who Lived In A Shoe
Five Children
Jack Spratt
Mrs Spratt
Mary Mary
Miss Muffet
Humpty Dumpty
Old Mother Hubbard
Little Bo Peep
Jack
Jill
Little Boy Blue
Queen Imagination
Billy Bingo
Witch Sycorax
Grimalkin
Lion
Monkey
Priest of HE
HE
Spirit of the Wood
Old King Cole
Loons
Gremlins
Dancers
Fiddlers
1st Minstrel
2nd Minstrel
3rd Minstrel
4th Minstrel

ACT I

ACT II

AUTHOR'S NOTE

This play may be very successfully performed by either a mixed or an all female cast and can involve up to seventy young people on stage.

The production load may be efficiently shared as there are a number of items that can be rehearsed as separate entities: the two dance sequences in Act I Scene 3 and Act II Scene 6 (which provide an opportunity for an enthusiastic choreographer to create two show-stoppers!), and the Gremlin fight in Act II Scene 4. This fight can be great fun and gives a group of energetic young people a chance to be involved. It could well be prepared by a judo club or, if this proves difficult or unsuitable, it can be replaced with no loss of impact by a gymnastic display to outer-space-type music. Sycorax could introduce this with:

> "Loons, you have done well. Imagination is safe in the dungeons
> of HE and HE is well-pleased with your work this day. Therefore,
> I have arranged a special treat for you—behold!"

followed by the acrobatic display to music, at the end of which Sycorax continues with: "Now let me see . . ." etc. The minstrel's performance in Act II Scene 6 also provides an opportunity for sharing the production load.

SCENERY

The scenery can be very simple; the visual effectiveness of the scenes will depend upon imaginative lighting and costume.

For the **Land of Nursery Rhyme** two free-standing flats are suggested both with doors. Jack Spratt's house requires a practical window as well. The framework should be of 2 × 1 timber and covered with hessian which is then fireproofed (first contact your local Fire Officer for advice) and painted. The struts at the back (hinged for easy storage) will need weights on the horizontals. The shoe-shape may be made with hardboard additions. Logs are very easily made using an oblong box (e.g. an orange box) which is shaped by fixing chicken-wire around it and then covering with hessian and paint.

The wall for Act I Scene 2 is simply a hardboard-covered box-frame on castors.

All that is required for the **Court of Imagination** is a raised throne made other-worldly by ingenuity. Do not clutter your stage and impede your dancers. Imagination gently rocking on a suspended swing or trapeze whilst the dancers perform beneath her is very effective.

The **Cave of Witch Sycorax** requires a chest, a cauldron which "grows legs", and a transformation chamber, all of which are very straightforward. The chest should be begged, borrowed or hired. The cauldron can be made round with chicken-wire and papier mâché but without a bottom. Grimalkin can hide in this and, at the appropriate moment, he stands up and carries the cauldron like a skirt around himself across to Sycorax. This is very useful also for concealing a light for the effects when the spells are chanted. Alternatively, the cauldron may be simply a free-standing flat, supported with back-struts, which Grimalkin hides behind and picks up to move across to Sycorax. The transformation chamber may be embellished to suit requirements but it is based upon a cupboard with an escape route from the back which should lead to an area concealed by curtains or flaps extending from the sides of the cupboard.

COSTUMES

The costumes will depend upon resources and the ideas of the producer. However, suggestions for the Loons, HE, Septimus, Humpty Dumpty and Billy Bingo may be welcome.

The **Loons** are perhaps best kept simple: black tights and leotards, hair concealed under "nets" made from old tights or stockings. The character is conveyed with pop-eyes made by cutting a table-tennis ball in half with a razor-blade (make sure the edges of the two halves are not sharp) and making holes in the two halves through which to see. The two halves have fine elastic threaded through them which is joined to make a circle. This contraption is strapped around the head with the two half-balls over the eyes. Long green nails made with cardboard and fixed to the fingers with sticky tape complete the effect. Don't forget to ask your Loons to make two or three sets of eyes and fingernails each as accidents always happen just before they are due on stage.

HE should make an impact when he enters. It must be immediately clear that he represents television. This can be done with a box over the head from which a "TV screen" is cut on three sides. The character may wear a huge polka-dot bow-tie which might have associations for the audience with a well-known television personality!

Septimus requires a hairy wig under which he has a bald head. He has to be fitted with four more legs to add to his natural legs and arms. I suggest that these four be attached, two each, to the wrists at one end and to the body of the costume at the other end. When the spider enters, he has his arms raised, creating the eight-legged effect. The arms may then be dropped and used more effectively to gesticulate. This will give the impression of eight moving legs as opposed to the static effect of four legs fixed to the back of the actor.

Humpty Dumpty should be contrived with the face free otherwise the impact of the actor's performance will be diminished. If you think in terms of a walking egg, this will be difficult. The most effective idea I have encountered was to have the character bald; his bulk was conveyed by attaching a plastic hoop to the top of a pair of baggy trousers. To this hoop, a harness was attached which rested on the actor's shoulders. A blouse with a ruff-collar over the top of the harness and hoop completed the clown-like effect.

Billy Bingo can be effectively conveyed with a tabard on which are sewn numbers as on a bingo card.

SOUND EFFECTS
Sound effects can be recorded from BBC sound effects records, a free
catalogue of which is available on request from French's Theatre Bookshop.

Theatrical maroons may be purchased from theatre suppliers or firework
companies. They should be handled with great care and the advice of your
local Fire Officer should be sought and strictly followed. Maroons are great
fun and well worth the effort.

In conclusion, I trust that it is clear that the reference in Act I Scene 5 to
the final solution of the schoolteacher problem is in no way meant to be a
comment on the idea of Comprehensive Education, but on the unimagina-
tive application of that idea. In fact, the play was written and performed
whilst I was teaching at a Comprehensive school and the laughter at the line
was very heartfelt and uninhibited!

Brian L. Bishop

ACT I*

SCENE 1

The Land of Nursery Rhyme

There is a piano medley of nursery rhymes. Then the CURTAIN *rises to reveal Jack Spratt's house* UL, *which has a practical door and window, a large shoe-house* C, *which has a practical door, and a log downstage* R. *(See the Author's Note)*

General birdsong is heard, including a cuckoo call

Simple Simon enters. He stretches and yawns. The cuckoo is heard again. Simple Simon moves downstage and addresses the audience

Simple Simon Hello. I'm Simple. You can tell I'm Simple to be up and about so early while everyone else is in bed. Although what's so smart about lying in bed of a morning I don't know. Hark at those birds. I wouldn't be able to hear them if I were asleep in bed, now would I?

Wee Willie Winkie enters

Wee Willie Winkie (*yawning*) Hello, Simon, haven't you gone to bed yet?
Simple Simon Gone to bed? But it's morning, Wee Willie Winkie. I've only just got up.
Wee Willie Winkie Oh Simon, you're so simple it's really not worth talking to you—good-night.

Wee Willie Winkie exits

Simple Simon Good-night, Willie. What do I mean—good-night? I'm not that simple; it's morning. There's something very odd going on around here you know—people are acting very strangely. Take Willie for example. That's the second time this week that he's missed his rounds and he used to be so punctual. And everyone's so lethargic (that's not a bad word for a simpleton is it?)—all this lying in bed. It never used to be like this; there used to be hustle and bustle about the place, everyone was busy and happy to be up and doing in the mornings.

Septimus the spider enters

Septimus Hi Simon. Have you seen Little Miss Muffet this morning?
Simple Simon Hello Septimus. No, I haven't but she should be along

---

*N.B. Paragraph 3 on page ii of this Acting Edition regarding photocopying and video-recording should be carefully read.

shortly for her curds and whey. I'll tell you what, you hide behind that log and we'll give her a fright. This place needs livening up.

Septimus Well I'll have a go, but I don't seem to be able to frighten people any more. Do you—do you think I'm as hairy as I used to be?

Simple Simon Of course you are. I've never seen a hairier spider. Now you get behind there and we'll have some fun.

There is shouting from inside the shoe. Septimus hides behind the log

Oh no! That's the end of a peaceful morning. If that lot are getting up, I'm clearing off.

Simple Simon exits. The door to the shoe opens and the Old Woman chases out five ragamuffin Children

Old Woman Outside all of you. It's enough to drive a body to distraction. How I'm expected to cope with a squabbling mob like you in one tiny shoe I do not know. One, give Three her book back, and Five, if I catch you pulling Two's hair again I'll give you such a hiding ...

Children (*together*) {
But it was her ...
He won't let me share his sweets ...
She keeps pinching me ...
Give me back my marbles ... (*etc. etc.*)
}

The window of Jack Spratt's house opens and Jack Spratt appears

Jack Spratt Be quiet, you little horrors! There are people trying to get some sleep around here.

Old Woman Why, how dare you! Don't talk to my children like that, Jack Spratt—you great streak of ...

Jack Spratt Careful, careful—now watch your tongue. I've had cause to complain about you to the Residents' Association before. You've got a tongue as coarse as a hobnail boot. Still, what can you expect of someone who lives in a shoe?

Old Woman Now you listen here ...

Jack Spratt No, you listen here. They should never have let you move that shoe in the first place. It lowers the tone of the whole neighbourhood. If you must live in a shoe, do it somewhere else.

The door to the Spratts' house opens and Mrs Spratt comes out

Mrs Spratt (*to Jack*) Get back in, you.

Jack Spratt (*doing so*) Yes, dear.

Jack Spratt exits

Old Woman Oh, he's sent the cart horse out now, has he?

Mrs Spratt Cease, peasant; you are beneath my contempt. Back to your boot.

Old Woman Shoe if you don't mind!

Mrs Spratt I do mind, I mind very much.

Old Woman Too bad—TUBS!

Mrs Spratt (*flying at her*) You trollop!

They fight. Music from the "William Tell Overture"

Mary Mary, Miss Muffet, Humpty Dumpty, Old Mother Hubbard and Little Bo Peep all rush in and join in the fight

At the climax, Septimus jumps out from behind the log

Septimus Boo!

Silence as they all regard Septimus with curiosity

Boo?

Mary Mary That's all we need, some dumb spider "booing" all over the place. What's wrong with you anyway? Why can't you run away and catch flies like a normal spider?

Septimus But I am not a normal spider, that's the whole point.

Miss Muffet Oh Septimus, don't be upset, come over here and sit by me.

Septimus Don't talk like that to me. I am not your pet. You are supposed to be frightened of me! Don't you even know your own nursery rhyme?

> "There came a big spider
> And sat down beside her
> And frightend Miss Muffet away."

That's me—the big spider.

Miss Muffet Oh I couldn't be frightened of you, Septimus.

Septimus (*taking out a mirror*) Why not—you think I'm losing my hair?

Miss Muffet No, of course you're not losing your hair, it's just that—well we've been together for such a long time and . . .

Septimus But you can pretend can't you? For the sake of our rhyme you can pretend.

Miss Muffet Oh what's the use of pretending?

Septimus What's the use of pretending! You—a nursery-rhyme character— ask a question like that? Wow! Something's really gone wrong with this place.

Old Woman You can say that again; if we're all standing around listening to a spider telling us that something's gone wrong, we must be crazy. "Something's gone wrong!" Of course something's gone wrong: the price of houses being what it is, I'm forced to bring up a family in a shoe— that's what's wrong.

Humpty Dumpty Madam, raise your mind above the level of your own trouble, do. Septimus is quite right. There is a general evil to which we must address ourselves: "Something is rotten in the State of Denmark".

Old Woman OK egghead, you're very clever, although what you are talking about Denmark for I don't know. But if something is as wrong as you say it is—what is it?

Old Mother Hubbard I'll tell you what it is—it's not the price of houses, it's the price of food. Do you know, I haven't got a thing in the house—my poor dog is starving too.

Humpty Dumpty Your dog! Really, if I might be permitted to say so, Old Mother Hubbard, you are falling into the the same trap as our friend here. What we are facing is of far greater proportions than a shoe or a dog. What we are facing is a crisis.

Little Bo Peep He's right.

Mrs Spratt Oh is he? You can't even look after a flock of sheep without losing them, so just why we should be impressed by what you say, I can't think.

There are cries from off

Oh no! This used to be a peaceful neighbourhood (*Staring with meaning at the Old Woman*) But what can you expect? Let one in and in come their friends.

Jack and Jill enter crying. They are holding a bucket between them with one hand and their heads with the other

Mary Mary Oh be quiet can't you! Every day it's the same. We know, we know. You were going up this hill to fetch a pail of water when Jack fell down causing you to lose your balance whereupon you both rolled to the bottom of the hill incurring multiple contusions and lacerations to your respective crowns in the process. Am I right?

Jill Well Mary, something like that, yes.

Jack There was a time when we used to get a sympathetic hearing for our story. What's wrong with you anyway? Why are you so contrary lately? Have you got a bad attack of greenfly in your precious garden?

Mary Mary All those tumbles down your stupid hill must have addled your brains. Silver bells and cockle shells have a built in resistance to greenfly—one of the little-known reasons why I grow them as a matter of fact.

Jill Well why are you so grumpy then?

Mary Mary This place is a bore. Nobody comes here any more. I'm fed up with the same old faces, the same old routine.

Humpty Dumpty Mary is right and I think that she has expressed our problem very well—"nobody comes here any more". But why? That is the question we have to answer. Our land which was once a tourist attraction is so no longer; our streets that were once thronging with happy, laughing children are now empty. Why? Where are we going wrong?

Little Boy Blue enters and gives a blast on his horn

Little Boy Blue All nursery-rhyme characters are summoned to the Court of Imagination immediately, where an extraordinary general meeting is to be held to discuss the nature of and possible remedies for, the evil that has overtaken us.

Little Boy Blue exits

There is general excitement

Humpty Dumpty The Court of Imagination! This is really serious. The last time there was a general meeting called there, it was to discuss the possible merger of all nursery rhymes into a common European edition. I suggest we all hurry along—momentous decisions are about to be made.

They all exit excitedly, leaving only Septimus

Septimus Momentous decisions! The only momentous decision I'm interested in is how to stop my hair falling out. It's no joke. Being a black spider makes it worse you see—well the dandruff! It shows up something shocking. I've tried that Head and Shoulders but it's no good. Not for spiders anyway. It's all very well saying you shouldn't wear black, but you can't change your nature can you? Oh well—I might as well follow the others I suppose. Don't go away—I'll be around in a minute.

Septimus exits

There is a piano nursery-rhyme medley as the tabs close

SCENE 2

On the way to the Court of Imagination

Humpty Dumpty enters in front of the tabs

Humpty Dumpty It can't be far now. I'll rest awhile on this wall. (*After a pause, louder*) Yes! That's what I'll do. I'LL REST AWHILE ON THIS WALL.

A wall is thrust through the tabs (see the Author's Note)

Now, if you're expecting me to fall off and to break into a thousand pieces whilst King's Horses and Men rush on and try to put me together again, you show a creditable knowledge of nursery rhyme but, if you'll forgive me, a rather naïve sense of the theatre. No, they're changing the scene and they stick me out here in the hope that you won't notice. Clever really isn't it!

Septimus enters

Septimus Oh, Humpty Dumpty. Thank goodness I've found you.
Humpty Dumpty Hello, Septimus. What do you mean, thank goodness you've found me! You've only just left me.
Septimus Ah, but you were with a crowd of people, then. What I have to say is of rather a delicate nature.
Humpty Dumpty Well you've come to the right person, Septimus. I'm of rather a delicate nature myself. (*He taps his shell*) That's a yoke.

Septimus groans

I see you're in a serious mood. Well what's troubling you?
Septimus Hair.
Humpty Dumpty Hair? Well now, hair is something that doesn't bother me at all.
Septimus Exactly. That is why I wanted to speak to you in particular.
Humpty Dumpty Explain yourself.
Septimus Well, you'll forgive me, but . . . well, to speak plainly, you've not a

hair on your head—or anywhere else come to that—and, as you say yourself, it doesn't bother you at all.

Humpty Dumpty Quite right, but get to the point—you're becoming boring.

Septimus Well, I was wondering if you could impart some of your philosophy to me, if, in short, you can help me to live with . . . falling hair.

Humpty Dumpty Falling hair! But I've never seen a hairier creature! In fact, I was thinking only last week that, if anything, you are hairier than you were last year.

Septimus Oh dear. . . . You noticed. I was afraid it might show. (*He removes a wig to reveal his bald head*)

Humpty Dumpty A wig . . . ha, ha, ha. A spider with a wig . . . ho, ho, ho. I've seen it all now.

Septimus There—I knew you'd laugh.

Humpty Dumpty But you mustn't be so sensitive.

Septimus But I am sensitive. It's no use saying it doesn't matter when you burst out laughing at me. And you're right: it's ludicrous—whoever heard of a bald spider?

Humpty Dumpty My dear chap, I wasn't laughing at you for being bald, after all it's a mark of distinction. No, what does strike me as rather amusing though is that you feel it necessary to cover it up with a wig. It's all in the mind, old boy. Hair means different things to different people— listen:

A monk will shave his head when he becomes a brother,
Hair's the way the hippies recognize one another,
A baby born today can't tell his father from his mother.
It's all in the mind.
Hair upon the chin some people think delightful
To praise someone on their moustache is thought to be politeful.
Unless of course you're female, in which case it's quite spiteful.
It's all in the mind.
The fashions change from day to day I pay them slight attention.
A style which shocks the world today will soon become convention.
So even though you're topless now it's scarcely worth a mention.
It's all in the mind!

Septimus Well maybe you're right; all the same I think I'll keep the wig on. You will respect my confidence of course.

Humpty Dumpty But of course, old boy—after all we're going to the Court of Imagination so you imagine that that beautiful head of hair is all your own work if that makes you happy.

Septimus and Humpty Dumpty exit

SCENE 3

The Court of Imagination

The tabs part to reveal Queen Imagination, seated on a raised throne (see

Author's Note), and all the characters from the Land of Nursery Rhyme watching a dance

Imagination My faithful servants—welcome to you all. You are no doubt wondering why I have called you all together like this. I wish to confide in you, to seek your advice. You must all be aware that our land is not the happy laughing place it used to be but a short while ago. We are no longer visited daily by crowds of excited children as we once were. Occasionally a solitary child will wander through our countryside with a bored, lost look upon his face, only to hurry away again as quickly as possible. Why is this? Where are we going wrong? These are questions which you have, no doubt, asked yourselves. It has been brought to my attention that you are beginning to blame one another and that this is giving rise to quarrels amongst yourselves. For this reason I have decided to address you today. My friends, an evil influence is at work and I have to tell you that the Land of Childhood is under a spell.

Gasps

Whilst visiting there the other day in an attempt to discover why my influence was declining, I found that the whole population was entranced; no-one recognized me; they were all under the dominion of a hideous monster.

Jill Your Majesty, what did this monster look like? Where did it come from? How has it managed to usurp your place as Queen of the Land of Childhood?

Imagination One question at a time, Jill. I cannot tell you where the monster comes from, I can only tell you that it was born in an evil hour. It is indescribably ugly, but it is able to change its appearance and then hypnotize its unfortunate victims into blind obedience.

Little Bo Peep Maybe we could capture it and tame it. It sounds as if it would make a very good job of looking after my sheep.

Imagination Sheep are what the inhabitants of the Land of Childhood have become, Bo Peep.

Little Boy Blue But what are we to do, Your Majesty? We cannot allow this situation to continue. How are we to break this tyrant's power?

Simple Simon Might I be permitted to make a suggestion, Your Majesty?

Imagination By all means, Simple Simon.

Old Woman Ah, the brain comes to our rescue!

Jack Spratt Don't be so rude. You're a one to talk about brains. It's hardly the most intelligent thing in the world to have so many children that you don't know what to do.

Mrs Spratt Be quiet, husband. The best way to treat such trash is to ignore it.

Old Woman Trash indeed! You fat-swallowing rubbish bin, I——

Little Boy Blue (*with a blast on his horn*) You forget yourselves.

Imagination Thank you, Little Boy Blue. An example of the lack of harmony between us I think. Simon, I believe you were about to make a suggestion.

Simple Simon Oh . . . er . . . was I? Oh dear . . . I'm afraid I've forgotten
  what it was.
Imagination Never mind, Simon. Thank you anyway for trying to help.
Humpty Dumpty Your Majesty, if I might be permitted to speak.

Imagination nods

  You say that the Land of Childhood is in the power of a hideous monster;
  that through some witchcraft this wretch has hypnotized everyone there
  so that they obey no-one but him.
Imagination That, I am afraid, is the case, Humpty Dumpty.
Humpty Dumpty It would therefore seem that the task before us is to
  discover this monster's lair, capture it and force it to render the dominion
  of the Land of Childhood to you, to whom it rightly belongs.

Mutters of agreement

Imagination Humpty Dumpty is right. That is indeed our task. But I am
  afraid it is far easier stated than carried out. You see the monster, who is
  referred to by his followers as HE, is protected by an ugly old witch and
  her helpers, the revolting Bug-eyed Loons. They have agents everywhere
  and whenever the power of HE is threatened they have a way of knowing
  and preventing it. Why, there may even be one of their agents here now,
  listening to our plans.

Upheaval

Mary Mary I, personally, wouldn't be at all surprised. (*Advancing on
  Septimus*) For some time now I've had my suspicions about this hairy
  creature. He's pretty sneaky—jumping out on people all the time. Come
  to think of it—Bug-eyed Loon's not a bad description of him.
Septimus Hairy! She called me hairy! Oh, thank you! Thank you! Thank
  you! That's the nicest thing that's been said to me all week.
Miss Muffet (*putting her arms around Septimus*) Ah poor Septimus. How
  can you be so unkind to him?
Septimus Don't do that!
Imagination You misunderstand me, Mary. I do not for one moment
  suspect any of the inhabitants of spying, only a soulless oaf would work
  for Witch Sycorax. Unfortunately, she has many of these at her command
  and they are very vigilant.
Wee Willie Winkie Well, with respect, Your Majesty, if one of Witch
  Sycorax's agents is here right now, he will not have learnt very much
  about our plans, as we know very little about them ourselves.
Imagination Quite right, Wee Willie Winkie. You do well to remind us of
  our purpose. My friends, action, and action of the most daring kind is
  called for. I need two volunteers for a most dangerous mission. It is
  essential that these two volunteers visit the Land of Childhood and track
  the monstrous HE to his hiding place. They must then bring word to me
  and we will construct a plan to isolate him there and overpower him.
Simple Simon Your Majesty, let me go. Why the Land of Childhood is a

jolly place and nursery-rhyme characters are welcome there. I would not be afraid to go to the Land of Childhood.

Old Woman I object. Old half-conscious there, always supposing he didn't get lost on the way, would forget what he had gone for as soon as he arrived.

Disapproval

Imagination Old Woman, you have a harsh tongue! However, Simon, I am afraid you do not fully appreciate the situation. There are few hearts that would welcome you in the Land of Childhood today. You could not rely upon being sheltered there now. You would have to survive by your wits and I am sure you will understand if I say that you will serve us best by staying in the Land of Nursery Rhyme. Old Woman, if your wits are as sharp as your tongue, you should do very well. Would you care to volunteer?

Old Woman Oh well . . . of course, Your Majesty, I should be delighted to serve you in any way possible. But—the children—what would they do without me?

Children Oh we don't mind; please go. (*etc. etc.*)

Old Woman Silence! You see what I mean? I am afraid they would never allow it.

Imagination Yes, I see. Your sense of duty is highly commendable.

Septimus Your Majesty, I am the fellow for the job. Please allow me to go. I would like to see any Bug-eyed Loon get in my way!

Miss Muffet Oh Septimus. You dear brave little spider! But no-one could be afraid of you.

Septimus Look—I've told you before. Don't talk to me like that in front of all these people! The only reason you aren't afraid of me is that I've allowed you to get too friendly with me that's all. I should have kept you at a proper distance. To anyone who's never seen me before I'm a pretty scary individual. Now don't under-estimate me.

Imagination Thank you, Septimus, for volunteering: I do appreciate it very much. But, as you say yourself, you are a pretty fearsome creature and anyone in the Land of Childhood, confronted with a hairy individual like yourself, is likely to scream the place down and give the game away altogether.

Septimus Your Majesty is so right. My, but I'm an ugly hairy brute. Oh well, "they also serve who only stand and wait".

Humpty Dumpty Noble sentiments, Septimus, noble sentiments.

Jill Your Majesty, my brother and I would like to volunteer for the mission you have in mind. We feel that we most resemble two people from the Land of Childhood and therefore would not draw attention to ourselves as some of the more distinctive characters might.

Jack That's right, Your Majesty. Just tell us what we have to do—so long as there are no hills to climb—we are at your service.

Imagination Well Jack and Jill, I think you would both do very well. My plan is this: you must slip into the Land of Childhood tonight under the cover of darkness. Once there, you will have to wait until tomorrow evening when all the children come out of school. Look for a child with a glazed look in his eyes. Such a child will not be hard to find and it is a sure sign that the child is under the influence of HE. Follow this child and you will be led to the monster's altar. There you must stay, witnessing the sickening spectacle of the child's abject slavery until HE, having proved the loyalty of his slave, retires for the night. It is then that you must be most alert. The monster must be tracked and as soon as you have discovered his evil dwelling-place, you must return and we shall devise a plan to ensnare HE and release the Land of Childhood from his devilish power.

Jack Come, sister—we must waste no time. Our journey is a long one and we must reach the boundaries of the Land of Childhood before nightfall. Farewell, Your Majesty—we shall return.

Jill Goodbye, everyone—wish us luck.

All Goodbye. Good luck. (*etc.*)

Imagination Now, my friends—you must all depart, and remember—you may be watched. So do not discuss our plans. Behave normally and we will meet here in two days' time.

All, except Imagination, exit

(*Moving downstage*) I fear the journey will be more hazardous than my brave countrymen realize. So long as I remain free, my influence will guide them to the Land of Childhood, but if our plan is discovered and I am ensnared, they will never find their way there.

There is ominous music as the tabs close

SCENE 4

On the way to the Cave of Witch Sycorax

Billy Bingo enters cackling, in front of the tabs

Billy Bingo   My name is Billy Bingo,
I'm a charming little sprite.
I bring you relaxation
Almost any day or night.
The lights are low, the game's begun,
You cannot hear a murmur.
All eyes on me, it's so much fun,
What's this? An eager learner.

Why come in, friend, no don't turn back,
Inside it's warm and cosy.
Give me your coat, and now your mind
And now your future's rosy.
And if when you emerge you find
The world is just as lousy,

> You can always close your eyes
> Or just shout Housey Housey.

Yes, Billy Bingo's my name and I serve Witch Sycorax and her Bug-eyed Loons. Imagination does well to fear us for we are out to destroy her. Let Imagination wander freely in the world and the future for characters such as me is very bleak indeed. I've just come from her palace—I heard it all. What a puny little plan. It shall be prevented. The Land of Childhood must be protected from a free imagination. I must hurry to my mistress the ugly old witch Sycorax. Wait till I tell her that Imagination called her ugly: she will be furious! She will spare no effort to see Imagination in chains.

Billy Bingo exits

Scene 5

The Cave of Witch Sycorax

There is a transformation chamber, besom broom and chest upstage and a stool and cauldron C. *(See the Author's Note)*

The tabs part to reveal Sycorax and her cat Grimalkin who is reading a paper

Sycorax Grimalkin—I'm bored. The botton has fallen right out of the wicked witchcraft business. HE has got the Land of Childhood so completely sewn up that there's absolutely nothing to do. When did we last hear of anyone showing a spark of imagination that had to be stamped out? Imagination has lost the battle for the Land of Childhood and we are redundant. Cat! I am addressing you—kindly show some interest, you mangy mog.
Grimalkin Well as far as I'm concerned, old hag, this is the life! Admittedly, the company leaves much to be desired, but loafing around suits me fine.
Sycorax Just what I would expect from you, you insolent feline. Why I keep you, I don't know, for two frogs' legs I'd turn you into a black rat.
Grimalkin Watch it, lady! You without me are nothing! Whoever heard of a witch without a cat? And remember, I haven't hung around this joint for five hundred years without learning a trick or two myself so if you've any ideas about messing around with me, forget them, or maybe I'll amuse myself with that witch in the bottle trick!
Sycorax Bah! You make me tired. Where are those wretched Bug-eyed Loons? Let's see what they have to report. (*She goes* L; *calling*) Loons! (*She goes* R; *calling*) Loons!

The Loons enter

Which of you can bring me news that will cheer me? My, but you're an ugly sight! Let's hope that your words are more attractive than your revolting exteriors. You three, what news from the Land of Architects?
1st Loon Nothing to report, O Sycorax.

2nd Loon No work to be done there: ugliness, most beautifully-designed ugliness, everywhere.

3rd Loon Not a sign of Imagination throughout the land.

1st Loon The architects are most enthusiastically on our side, Sycorax. Everywhere they are designing great temples to ugliness.

2nd Loon Wherever there is a vista that would delight the foolish heart of man, there an architect, fired with a zeal that even you would be forced to admire, is to be found scheming and plotting its ruination.

3rd Loon From the Land of Architects, O Sycorax, we can report a total absence of Imagination's influence.

Sycorax Bah—I need a challenge. The wretched architects were no test for my power. You three—what of the Land of Politicians?

4th Loon Ah, Sycorax! The Land of Politicians was your master-stroke.

5th Loon Sheer genius led you to capture that land for HE.

6th Loon HE will be eternally grateful to you for the job you have done in the Land of Politicians.

4th Loon An unbelievable lack of imagination pervades every square inch of the land.

5th Loon The politicians' influence is such that the whole world of Man is deadened by their presence.

6th Loon Nothing but a great yawn to report from the Land of Politicians, O Sycorax.

Sycorax Heh! Heh! As I thought, just as I thought. A very tame bunch. Imagination stands no chance there. You say that the whole world of Man reponds to their deadening influence. Tell me more of that.

7th Loon The world of Man is inspired, there is no other word for it, inspired by a monumental lack of Imagination.

8th Loon You, O Sycorax, even you would be moved by the readiness with which Man poisons his rivers, fouls his air, cuts down his trees.

9th Loon Everywhere foulness, everywhere ugliness. O Sycorax, your wizened old heart would rejoice to see it.

7th Loon But best of all to observe is the treatment of those who would take Imagination's side.

8th Loon Nobody listens to them: they are ignored.

9th Loon They are regarded as fools—madmen. O Sycorax, the world of Man is ours.

Sycorax But what of the future? The biggest threat lies in the Land of Childhood. HE has captured that but can it be held? It is on the Land of Childhood that Imagination will make her strongest counter-attack. Therefore, we must keep a vigilant watch on those who have influence there.

10th Loon No problem there, O Sycorax. Not a spark of imagination to be found.

11th Loon There is a story of which we can all be proud; Imagination will not be aided in the Land of Schoolteachers.

12th Loon Unbelievable, O Sycorax is the foolishness of schoolteachers.

10th Loon So vast are the schools that they have created that Imagination herself gets lost in their corridors.

11th Loon So great is the bulk of paper used to pass messages to one another that the imagination of hundreds of schoolteachers is crushed beneath its weight each week.

12th Loon O Sycorax, the Land of Schoolteachers is a pretty sight.

10th Loon We are far advanced with our plan for the final solution of the schoolteacher problem.

11th Loon One day soon we shall herd them all into a colossal Comprehensive school.

12th Loon Then we shall lock all the doors and throw the key away.

10th Loon And all the schoolteachers in the land will spend eternity passing messages to one another on little pieces of paper.

Sycorax You have done well, my ugly brethren. The grip that HE has on the Land of Childhood would seem to be secure. One report remains to be heard—that of Billy Bingo from the Land of Nursery Rhyme where resides Imagination herself. Unless he has news of a counter-attack from there, it seems I am to remain bored, Grimalkin. What's this you are reading? (*She snatches his paper away*) *The Witch's Familiar's Weekly*. What trash is this? Full of articles telling you how to annoy your mistress no doubt. (*She throws it back*)

Grimalkin Relax, old hag. Here, if you're so bored, how about trying this. Listen: (*reading*) "Cats—are you puny? Undernourished? Do dogs kick earth in your eyes? Your worries are over with this new wonder spell that your old hag can work for you:

> Take one worm that has turned
> Finely chop and add one last straw
> Flavour with the final insult
> And gently infuse in righteous indignation.

Have her stir the mixture thoroughly and mutter the following:

> "Pussy cat, pussy cat, bustle and hustle,
> Eyes down and looking for an increase in muscle."

Well how about that, Sycorax—do you think you could manage a bit of body-building on my behalf?

Sycorax Huh. Show me a spell that I cannot work—Loons! Fetch the ingredients.

The Loons exit

Now, cat, enter the transformation chamber. Heh! Heh! I've been wanting to get you in there for ages.

Grimalkin Listen, old mother, I've got friends and if they see a black rat running around here instead of me, they'll begin to get suspicious. Remember, you are not the only one with magical powers. So if you know what's good for you, you'll suppress your evil urges and make sure that I emerge from that box as feline as I went in—only more so. (*He enters the transformation chamber*)

Sycorax Relax, pusillanimous puss cat, and get into the box. (*She closes the door on Grimalkin*)

The Loons enter with the spell ingredients. Grimalkin exits

Ah, the ingredients. Loons, form a circle whilst I stir the mixture.

The Loons circle the cauldron while Sycorax stirs the mixture and recites the spell. At the same time, the Lights gradually fade to Black-out

> In the pot the contents throw
> Round and round the circle go.
> Magic from the air descend,
> Aid us now to help our friend.
> Change Grimalkin, let him be
> A cat for all the world to see.

At the climax of the spell a light concealed inside the cauldron flashes on and off to illuminate the Loons' faces in an eerie fashion. The Lights return to normal. There is a loud roar

GRIMALKIN! GRIMALKIN! Are you all right? Come out, nice pussy.

There is another loud roar

Grimalkin! Is that you inside there, Grimalkin? (*She opens the door of the transformation chamber*)

A Lion leaps out

Sycorax and the Loons withdraw

Lion Lord Grimalkin if you don't mind, old hag—Lord Grimalkin. King of the Underworld.
Sycorax Arh! that'll be the day. Lord Grimalkin, King of the Underworld indeed? Over my dead body.
Lion Exactly what I had in mind. Loons, tie her up.
Sycorax No, indeed you shall not! Stay, where you are all of you or else I shall turn you into beetles.
Lion Ignore her, fools, or else I shall make a bug-eyed loon fricasee out of you. She is powerless. This place is under new management from now on.
Sycorax Why do you turn on me like this, you heartless ungrateful beast? I did what you asked, more fool me. Why do you bite the hand that feeds you?
Lion Bite the hand that feeds me indeed! When did you last give me a decent meal, old hag? If you had not starved me for the last five hundred years, I would not have needed this new, power-packed body!
Sycorax I took you in and sheltered you when you were homeless and friendless.
Lion You sheltered me for your own ends, O ugly one. No self-respecting cat would stay with you for more than a decade. I hadn't a self that I could respect but now, ho! ho! there will be a few changes. (*He picks up the besom broom*) What about all those journeys riding pillion on this thing? You don't think this is luxury travel do you? Why, I ought to break it over your head.
Sycorax No, please Grimalkin, please put the transport down. It's a very delicate instrument and it's so difficult getting the spares nowadays ...

Lion Silence, hag! Loons, place Mother Ugly here in the transformation chamber.

The Loons put Sycorax in the transformation chamber

Sycorax Oh please, Grimalkin—spare me, spare me. Don't do anything rash, you'd only regret it, you know you would.
Lion Gag her!

She is gagged and the door of the transformation chamber closed on her

Sycorax exits

Right now, fetch me the book of "Spells for Rainy Saturdays". Ha! Ha! I've played second fiddle to that old crone for long enough, I've always wanted the lion's share of the business.

The spell book arrives

Now let me see—"Vindictive Spells". Ah yes, this is the section; I feel very vindictive today. (*Reading*) "To teach someone a lesson they will never forget, first of all lower the lights." That's easy. (*He flashes his fingers*)

There is a loud bang and a Black-out. The Lion moves to the front of the stage and shines a torch on the audience

Are you still there? I'm sorry about the bang—I've not got used to my own strength yet. Now let me see. (*Reading*) "To the accompaniment of spooky music—perform the dance of the enchanted lights." Now this could be a little awkward, you'll have to be very patient with me. (*He clears his throat*)
Dancing lights come to our aid.
Help us till the spell is made."

The Loons light torches

Now for the music:
"Grave of vampire split and rend
Unearthly music now descend."

There is music and the Loons perform the "Dance of Lights". (NB. Remember how effective it is to hold a lighted torch underneath the chin when the other lights are out)

That should have done the trick. Now to bring the lights back up—are you ready for the bang? One, two, three. (*He flashes his fingers*)

The Lights come up. Silence

That's funny—no bang.

There is a loud bang and the Lion collapses. The Loons make towards him and he rises angrily

Get away from me, you repulsive creatures. There's more to this magic than meets the eye. You could do yourself a nasty injury like that. (*He feels himself and looks at his tail*) I still seem to have everything. Right then—on with the show. (*He consults the book*) "Mutter the following magic word—British Telecom (*or similar topical allusion*)! Your victim should now be turned into her nearest relation." My goodness me, what a horrible fate! Honestly, I'm so wicked I sometimes shock myself. Right, Loons, open the door of the transformation chamber.

The Loons open the door

A Monkey leaps out

Oh no! I've bungled—I've improved you, old hag. By comparison you're quite attractive.

Monkey You great, muscle-bound beast—turn me back! You'll be sorry for this—you wait and see.

Lion But I can't—I don't know how to. It was one of your vindictive spells and as you know, the whole point of a vindictive spell is that you can't undo it.

Monkey You great, stupid lump. I'll get even with you. Why I'll, I'll ...

Lion You'll what? You're not a witch any longer—you're a monkey. All you'll do from now on is peel the odd banana. Ha! Ha! If you're a good little monkey I'll let you ride on my back.

Monkey Oohh! Loons, do something—don't just stand there gawping, you bug-eyed fools.

Lion You forget yourself, old hag: that is the function of a Bug-eyed Loon—to stand and gawp. HE has decreed that all Bug-eyed Loons shall, as a mark of respect, stand and gawp for at least seven hours each day.

Monkey HE—that's it! HE will aid me. HE will be most displeased with what you have done to this most devoted servant. I shall run to the temple of HE ...

Lion Wait! It was a joke, dear old mother—a joke. You don't want to bother HE with our little games. Now you just come back here—we'll sort everything out; there's no need to trouble HE.

Monkey Ah! Now you're singing a different tune, aren't you? But how, O great lumox, do you propose to undo the mischief that you have done? As you say, vindictive spells are almost impossible to undo!

Lion Don't worry. Don't you worry about one little thing, my furry little friend. Now you get back into the transformation chamber and leave everything to me.

Monkey I have little choice. But you'd better think fast, Lion, or else HE will hear of this, I promise you.

Lion Yes, yes. Now don't you worry. That's right. In you get now—patience, patience.

The Monkey gets into the transformation chamber and the Lion shuts the door

The Monkey exits

Oh what can I do! Where's that book of magic. Now let me see—"Antidotes"—here we are—"Vindictive Spells". (*Reading*) "Should you be foolish enough to wish to undo a vindictive spell, you will have to observe the following conditions: kick yourself heartily three times." Oh dear—well, I suppose I must. (*He does so*) Oh, how embarrassing. Loons, can't you stare somewhere else! Have you no mercy? Oh what's the use! Let's get on with it. (*Reading*) "Eat one humble pie."

A Loon exits

Oh no! I hate humble pie

The Loon enters with a pie

The pie could be made from "Crazy Foam", available from joke shops, which the Loon pushes into the Lion's face. Alternatively, it could be an ordinary pie which the Lion eats

Oh revolting, ugh, horrible. Oh dear! I'll never work a vindictive spell again. (*Reading*) "Bang your head on the floor three times and repeat the following: I'm a Charley, I'm a chump, on my head fetch up a lump." Oh the shame of it all, in front of all these people as well. (*Banging his head on the floor*) I'm a Charley, I'm a chump, on my head fetch up a lump. Oh! My poor head, oh never again, never again. Let's hope it worked at any rate. Loons, open the door.

They do so revealing:

Billy Bingo who steps out of the transformation chamber

Billy Bingo Here, here, here, what's all this then? Hello, isn't this the Cave of Sycorax?
Lion Yes, I'm afraid it is.
Billy Bingo Ooh! My life—a talking lion! Whatever next?
Lion It's me—Grimalkin. You know me, Billy.
Billy Bingo GRIMALKIN! What, that scrawny alley cat? I suppose you have been at the Weetabix?
Lion Steady on, Billy, I've had just about all I can stand. Look, I am Grimalkin but Sycorax and me have been fooling around with spells to pass the time. You see we get bored; there's nothing to do. HE has settled Imagination's hash once and for all.
Billy Bingo Oh, has he? What do you think I'm doing here? I've come to warn Sycorax that Imagination has launched a desperate counter-attack. Already two of her agents—Jack and Jill—are on their way to the Land of Childhood to track HE down.
Lion Oh dear, this is serious. And I've lost Sycorax. I turned her into a monkey and was trying to turn her back again when you appeared.
Billy Bingo So that's what happened! I wondered how I got here so quickly. I must have crossed the spell wave and caused a short circuit. Poor old Sycorax will be somewhere in Limbo!
Lion Just to think, I ate that humble pie for nothing. And it's given me the most awful indigestion.
Billy Bingo Now we've really got a problem. We must find Sycorax immediately or else my warning will be too late and all will be lost.

Quickly, you must go and find her—into the transformation chamber and don't come out until you have contacted her!

The Lion enters the transformation chamber and the door is closed on him

The Lion exits

Now then, Loons, we must assist by gathering all our powers of concentration together. If Imagination is allowed to wander, she will wreak havoc so—eyes down and looking.

They all perform a ritual dance around the cauldron as they chant and the Lights fade gradually to Black-out

All (*chanting*) On it's own number one, unlucky for some thirteen, clickety-click sixty-six, two fat ladies eighty-eight, dinky doo twenty-two, Downing Street number ten, key of the door twenty-one—BINGO!

As before, the light concealed inside the cauldron flashes on and off to illuminate the Loon's faces in an eerie fashion. The Lights return to normal

The door to the transformation chamber opens revealing Sycorax and Grimalkin. Sycorax chases Grimalkin from the chamber

Sycorax Why you bungling fool, I'll skin you alive.

Grimalkin Please, Sycorax, it wasn't my fault, it was Billy Bingo who interfered by crossing the spell wave.

Sycorax Billy? Why what are you doing here? Anything to report from the Land of Nursery Rhyme?

Billy Bingo Anything to report! I'll say there is. You have made your reappearance not a moment too soon. Why even now we may be too late. Imagination has sent Jack and Jill to the Land of Childhood in order to track down HE so that she may launch a counter-attack and reclaim the land of Childhood for herself.

Sycorax Oh dear, this is serious. What are we to do? If Imagination herself is guiding Jack and Jill, I am powerless to influence them. What's to be done?

Grimalkin Might I make a suggestion, old mother?

Sycorax It had better be a good one, mog.

Grimalkin We must journey to the temple of HE and enlist the help of the all-powerful. HE will know how to deal with Imagination.

Sycorax For once, O mangy one, you speak sense. This is a desperate measure that you suggest, but nothing else is left to us. Loons, prepare yourselves for the journey to the Temple of HE.

The Loons form up

Forward!

Chopin's Funeral March

Everyone exits

CURTAIN

ACT II

The Temple of HE

There is a dais upstage C

When the Curtain *rises church organ music plays and Sycorax, the Loons, Grimalkin and Billy Bingo are discovered kneeling and facing towards the dais*

The Priest of HE enters

Priest Welcome, faithful ones, to the Temple of HE. HE will be with us shortly but let us first compose ourselves. Empty your minds of all thought; forget that there is anyone else in the room with you. Surrender yourselves entirely to HE, King of the Land of Childhood, Conqueror of Imagination, the All-Powerful, your friend and my friend—HE.

The Priest holds up a card with APPLAUSE *written on it. The Loons do not applaud, but there is taped applause which is switched off abruptly. (Alternatively, this effect can be omitted and you can rely on audience response.) The music changes to an organ version of "Happy Days Are Hear Again"*

HE enters and goes to the dais. He is an animated TV set

There is obeisance from the Loons, Sycorax, Grimalkin, Billy Bingo and the Priest

HE Yes, friends, happy days are here again because every night is fun night with the good old TV. Is everybody happy?

All (*without expression*) Yes we are.

HE You lucky people. There's no need to budge from your old armchair. You can eat, sleep, and be royally entertained without moving a step. Is everybody happy?

All Yes we are.

HE You've never had it so good. I am your cinema, theatre, sports arena, church, all rolled into one. Is everybody happy?

All Yes we are.

HE (*descending from the dais and moving downstage* L) I should say so. Whatever would you do without me? Who would be so foolish as to contemplate life without HE—the good old TV?

Sycorax O master, there is such a one.

HE What? Someone speaks. Who dares give utterance in the presence of HE? Bring the rebel before me.

The Priest flings Sycorax at the feet of HE

You! Are you mad? When HE speaks all other communication ceases.

Sycorax But, master, you asked a question.

HE Fool! I ask questions as part of my entertainment programme—not that they should be answered. I am the master of the somnolent question. Nothing like a good question to send you to sleep. That is why I pose all the most serious questions last thing at night. See how solicitous HE is of your welfare?

Sycorax My master is most kind and considerate which is why I make so bold as to speak in his presence.

HE Explain, misshapen hag.

Sycorax Imagination is on the prowl.

HE Ha ha! Is that all? Who heeds Imagination? Let her prowl to her heart's content. I control the world of Man and no-one will be moved by Imagination.

Sycorax Imagination, O wise one, moves against the Land of Childhood.

HE A thousand curses on Imagination. The Land of Childhood is my Achilles' heel as she well knows. If she reclaims it, my future is bleak indeed.

Sycorax We await your command, master. Jack and Jill are, even now, making their way to the Land of Childhood that they may seek you out.

HE Jack and Jill can only find the way there whilst Imagination is free. She must be captured.

The Loons exhale "Ahh!" and turn downstage

Sycorax My loons are eager for the task, master. But where are we to find her?

HE Imagination is reputed to roam freely in the woodland at night. Long has this angered me for night time, as you know, is when I reign supreme. Let your ugly ones lay in wait for Imagination in the woodland tonight.

The Loons exhale "Ahh!" and advance downstage

Bind her in chains and bring her to me where she can rot in my dungeons. No longer will the world be troubled by an active imagination and my rule will be secure for ever.

HE exits upstage c

The tabs close quickly

Scene 2

The Woodland

There is the hoot of an owl

Imagination enters in front of the tabs

Imagination Ah me! My heart is very heavy and I am full of foreboding.

Jack and Jill have an awesome task before them and I sense that all is not well. I feel evil all around me and I fear that our plan has been discovered.

The tabs part to reveal a log and, C, a gaunt tree (free-standing) which has been blasted by lightning. In the dim light the Loons are seen frozen into grotesque shapes, each holding a tree branch in front of themselves as a rudimentary disguise. A spot illuminates the tree

(*Moving to the log*) Spirit of the Wood, sing me a melancholy song and I will rest a while upon this log.

The Spirit of the Wood enters and sings "Greensleeves". He exits at the end of the song

The air grows oppressive, I can hardly breathe; my limbs are weary, I must sleep. (*She lies down*)

There is thunder and lightning. The Lights dim further and the spotlight flashes on and off. The Loons become active: dropping their branches, they move towards Imagination as if through water

Imagination is bound and carried off by the Loons

The tabs close

SCENE 3

On the way to the Cave of Witch Sycorax

Billy Bingo and Grimalkin meet in front of the tabs

Billy Bingo They've done it, Grimalkin. The Loons have captured Imagination and taken her, bound to the temple of HE.

Grimalkin Yah! Tell me something interesting. I'm bored with the whole lousy business. You know, I think that you and I are a couple of fools.

Billy Bingo You speak for yourself, whiskers, personally, I am a pretty sharp character. Why, no-one pulls the wool over my eyes. I know just what's going on and I keep old Sycorax up to date with the very latest news.

Grimalkin Exactly my point, Bingo—why?

Billy Bingo What do you mean "Why"? Why what?

Grimalkin Well why do we waste our talents serving that ugly old witch Sycorax? I mean, what's in it for us?

Billy Bingo Well I've never really thought of an alternative. I've always served Sycorax.

Grimalkin Now come on, Billy, that's not very smart is it? "Because I've always done it" is not a very good reason for continuing to do something is it?

Billy Bingo You're in a very philosophical mood today. What's all this leading up to anyway?

Grimalkin Well, I suppose basically I'm not evil enough, Billy. You see I'm bored to tears half the time. Let's face it, it's not much fun being wicked is it? Take those characters in the Land of Nursery Rhyme for example.

Billy Bingo What, that bunch of Goody Goodies?

Grimalkin There you go you see. You feel you have to say that. You wouldn't be Billy Bingo unless you said that. But what does it matter what you call them? Who's getting the most fun out of life? That's the most important question.

Billy Bingo Bah, you're getting soft, Grimalkin.

Grimalkin You see—names again. You call me names because then you can avoid answering my question. Life should be fun; my life is not fun; their life seems to be fun; maybe I should try their way. Simple logic, old chap.

Billy Bingo That's—that's treason.

Grimalkin "Treason" another name you see. But what does treason mean? Disloyalty. Well is it such a bad thing to be disloyal to an evil old witch like Sycorax? Maybe we made a mistake when we agreed to serve her. So what you call "treason" could simply be correcting a mistake.

Billy Bingo Perhaps you're right. I must say, when I look around and see the effect I have on some people's lives, I get a twinge of conscience.

Grimalkin You see—you can't be properly evil either. You'd never find Sycorax or her Loons having a twinge of conscience.

Billy Bingo Well what's the use of talking like this? We can't do anything about it.

Grimalkin Oh yes we can.

Billy Bingo What do you propose?

Grimalkin I propose that we go to the cave of Sycorax; tell her that we are leaving her service and then try to undo some of our past evil by helping to release Imagination.

Billy Bingo You must be mad. You don't think Sycorax would let us go as easily as that do you? She would set her Loons on us.

Grimalkin Her Loons hold no fears for me—I know them too well. Threaten their aerials, Billy, and they are reduced to quivering jelly. Without their aerials they are cut off from the power of HE and then they are nothing.

Billy Bingo But why can we not just leave without telling Sycorax what we intend?

Grimalkin Because, Billy, I want to see her fume and rage. Five hundred years I have worked in her service. I cannot leave without seeing the look on her revolting face when I tell her that I am transferring my allegiance to Imagination.

Billy Bingo All right, Grimalkin, I am with you—lead on—I only hope you know what you are doing that's all.

Billy Bingo and Grimalkin exit

SCENE 4

The Cave of Witch Sycorax

The tabs part to reveal Sycorax's cave as before

Grimalkin is concealed either in or behind the cauldron C *(see the Author's Note). Sycorax is addressing the Loons*

Sycorax Loons, you have done well. Imagination is safe in the dungeons of HE and HE is well pleased with your work this day. Therefore, I have arranged a special treat for you—a gremlin fight.

The Loons exhale "Ahh!"

Wheel on the Green Gremlins.

Six Loons exit R *and then return, wheeling a cage of Green Gremlins*

As you know, these monsters are the deadly enemy of all Yellow Gremlins so—wheel on the Yellow Gremlins.

Six Loons exit L *and return, wheeling a cage of Yellow Gremlins*

The Gremlins rattle the bars of their cages

These are yours and these are yours. Let battle commence.

The respective groups of Loons release Gremlins and they fight (this could well be the judo club's contribution). Alternatively, a gymnastic display to music could take place here (see the Author's note)

Return them to their cages, Loons. Well have they fought. Wheel them off and throw them a bone to gnaw.

The Loons exit with the Gremlins

Now let me see. (*She picks up the spell book and sits on the stool*) Where is the new spell I was working on. (*Reading*) "Take from your store the essence of toad's liver." Ah, essence of toad's liver is kept in my chest.

She goes to the chest and, as she bends over it, the cauldron, where Grimalkin is hiding, "grows legs", follows her upstage and kicks her head first into the chest. Grimalkin returns C *with the cauldron*

(*Recovering herself*) What—who was that? Grimalkin—I know it was you—where are you? Come on out, you sneaky slob. (*She moves in front of the cauldron*)
Grimalkin (*leaping up*) Yaahh!
Sycorax (*collapsing to the ground*) You stupid animal; have you no respect? Why I'll see you on bread and water for a week for this.
Grimalkin (*climbing out of the cauldron*) Old hag, you'll see me on nothing! I'm resigning.
Sycorax You're what?

Grimalkin I'm resigning, I've finished serving you. We're through, I'm making a fresh start.

Sycorax You're making a fresh start! Why you dumb animal, how do you think you will survive without me? You need someone to look after you or you'd starve in no time.

Grimalkin I shall offer my services to Imagination—she will protect me.

Sycorax Ha! Ha! That's good—oh that's very good. Offer your services to Imagination, will you? Well you'll have to go to the dungeons of HE to do it, for that's where she lies, bound and helpless.

Grimalkin Bound she may be, but helpless she is not, for I and Billy Bingo will hasten to the Land of Nursery Rhyme and tell everyone what has happened to their queen. Together we shall think of a way to overcome your evil power.

Sycorax You traitorous pair. You shall not get away with this. You forget, cat, that here, I am queen. Stay where you are. Ha! Ha! It's a long time since I tried my beetle spell.

> "Cat to beetle let it be.
> Work, oh work, this spell for me,
> Black and furry pussy cat——"

The transformation chamber door opens and Billy Bingo rushes out

He grabs Sycorax and he and Grimalkin bustle her into the chamber and shut the door

Sycorax exits

Grimalkin Well done, Billy. She should be safe in there. (*Banging on the door*) Farewell, old mother—maybe in another five hundred years' time I'll drop in to see how you're managing without me.

Grimalkin and Billy Bingo exit laughing

The tabs close

SCENE 5

On the way to the Court of Old King Cole

Grimalkin and Billy Bingo enter in front of the tabs R

Grimalkin Are you sure you know where we are, Billy? There aren't many people about.

Billy Bingo This is the Land of Nursery Rhyme all right—there's no doubt about that, but why all the streets are deserted I do not know.

Grimalkin Perhaps they saw us coming and are plotting to give us an unpleasant welcome.

Billy Bingo No, they didn't see us coming. I've been getting in and out of this place for ages now without being spotted.

Grimalkin Hey!—that sounds like someone approaching—quickly behind here.

They hide behind proscenium arch L

   Jack and Jill enter R

Jack Well, Jill, we've let everybody down badly. We've completely failed in our mission.
Jill We didn't even find our way into the Land of Childhood. Oh! how could we be so stupid as to get lost!
Jack However are we going to face all our friends?

Grimalkin and Billy Bingo emerge from hiding

Grimalkin Excuse me, young sir.
Jack
Jill } *(together, startled)* Oh, who are you? What do you want?
Billy Bingo It's all right—we are your friends.
Jack Wait a minute—with that costume, you must be Billy Bingo.
Billy Bingo That's right.
Jill Then you're no friend of ours.
Jack You keep away from us; we know all about your evil ways.
Grimalkin No, please don't go—listen, we need your help. We're two reformed characters.
Billy Bingo We've left the service of Witch Sycorax and we've come to help everyone in the Land of Nursery Rhyme free Imagination.
Jack What do you mean free Imagination?
Grimalkin You're going too fast, Billy, let me explain. You see, Witch Sycorax and her Loons have captured Imagination and she lies bound in the dungeons of HE.
Jill Oh no! But that's awful. No wonder we got lost Jack. With Imagination in chains, we are helpless.
Jack We must do something at once! But what?
Grimalkin Well, the first thing is to tell everybody what has happened, but nobody is to be found. Do you know where they all are?
Jack Yes, everybody will be at the court of Old King Cole: every evening all Nursery Rhyme characters gather there for a party.
Grimalkin A party every night! You really have a good time in this part of the world, don't you?
Billy Bingo Well then, let's all go together—we've not a moment to lose.

   Everyone exits

SCENE 6

The Court of Old King Cole

The tabs part to reveal Old King Cole seated on a raised throne upstage and the nursery-rhyme characters, with the exception of Jack and Jill, watching the court Fiddlers perform a dance

Old King Cole Well done, well done, my friends. You are all doing your best to be cheerful but I think the time has come to ask the question that is at the back of everybody's mind—what has happened to Jack and Jill?

Murmurs

It's a week now since they set out for the Land of Childhood. They should have returned days ago. I fear for their safety.

Humpty Dumpty If I might make so bold, sir. I would like to draw your attention to the weather that we have been having lately.

Old Woman Listen clever Dick! The King is talking about Jack and Jill— what do you want to change the subject for?

Humpty Dumpty Madam, by your leave. I do not consider that I am changing the subject. The sun always shines in the Land of Nursery Rhyme.

Mary Mary Hooray! Now tell us something we don't know. That's the trouble with you intellectuals—you spend all your time stating the obvious.

Humpty Dumpty Quite so. Everyone knows that the sun always shines in our land—always that is until two days ago. The sky has been overcast with threatening storm clouds for two days. What, I ask myself, can this mean?

Simple Simon Rain.

Laughter

Humpty Dumpty Ah! Would that life were that simple, Simon. It is, I fear, an evil omen.

Old King Cole I think Humpty Dumpty is right. There is only one person who can help us solve our problems and that is Imagination. We must seek her out and crave an audience with her.

Grimalkin and Billy Bingo enter

Billy Bingo You will have to seek hard and far, King Cole.

The nursery-rhyme characters shrink away

Imagination lies bound in the dungeons of HE.

Old King Cole (*standing; commanding*) Billy Bingo and Grimalkin, servants of an evil master, how dare you enter my court!

Grimalkin We have come to offer our services to you. We no longer wish to waste our lives in the service of ugliness.

Billy Bingo We have decided that your life is much more fun so we have come to ask if we may join you.

Murmurs

Old King Cole Well, now there's a thing! Of course you can join us— everyone is welcome here. But how did you find your way to us?

Grimalkin We were shown the way by two friends of yours.

Jack and Jill enter

They are welcomed

Old King Cole Jack and Jill! Why, it is good to see you. But where have you been?

Jack I'm afraid we have let you down badly.

Jill You see, we got lost and we couldn't find our way into the Land of Childhood.

Jack You see, Sycorax and her Bug-eyed Loons have captured Imagination and she lies in chains in the Dungeons of HE.

Old King Cole This is indeed terrible news. No-one can find their way without Imagination. Unless she is kept free, we are lost.

Grimalkin Perhaps I can really prove that I mean to change my ways by making a helpful suggestion.

Old King Cole Helpful suggestions would be very welcome right now.

Grimalkin Well, I have spent five hundred years of my life trying to keep Imagination at bay and it has been a full time job because the moment anyone does something that requires Imagination, there she is.

Billy Bingo Yes, I can vouch for that. If Imagination was really needed before something could be done, then we were powerless to restrain her.

Grimalkin All we were able to do was discourage people from requiring Imagination's presence.

Old King Cole Of course, thank you for reminding us. Nothing could be simpler! In order to free Imagination, all we have to do is something imaginative.

Septimus Why don't you summon the minstrels and ask them to perform one of their stories? We really need Imagination when watching one of their performances.

Humpty Dumpty What a good idea, Septimus. We'll soon have Imagination out of the dungeons and with us once again.

Old King Cole Splendid—the very thing. Boy Blue, summon the minstrels.

Little Boy Blue gives a toot on his horn

The 1st Minstrel enters and bows

1st Minstrel You called, sir?

Old King Cole I did indeed, my friend. We've not had a story from your excellent company for a long while and we were wondering whether you could perform one for us now.

1st Minstrel Most certainly, sir. Had you a particular story in mind?

Old King Cole We thought perhaps one where we need to use a lot of imagination. One about an ogre would fit the bill.

1st Minstrel Most certainly, sir. If you would be so good as to take your places.

The 1st Minstrel exits R

Old King Cole (*coming down from his throne*) Right you are, everyone, take your places

They all retire R *and* L

Simple Simon Oh goody! Minstrels! I love stories.
Mary Mary "Oh goody—I love stories!" Wouldn't it make you sick.

Four Minstrels enter R, *pushing a handcart upon which are the properties they require for the following sequence. They are led by the smallest of them, the 4th Minstrel, who is beating a drum which is around his neck*

Drum roll

1st Minstrel There was once an ugly and terrible ogre who hated everyone.

The 2nd Minstrel takes a mask and stool from the cart and seats himself downstage R *as the Ogre*

All day long he paced up and down in his castle fuming and seething with hatred.

Fuming and seething, the Ogre gets up, crosses to L *and back to the stool again*

So full of hatred was he that his fame spread far and wide until, one day, his name appeared in *Ye Guinness Book of Records.*

Drum roll

This made the ogre very happy and proud,

The Ogre swells with pride

that in all the world there was nobody as full of hatred as he. However, on the other side of the world, in a place known as the Antipodes, there dwelt a very learned philosopher.

The 3rd Minstrel takes a beard, book and stool from the cart and sits downstage L *as the Philosopher*

All day long this wise sage sat studying the mysteries to be found in *Ye Guinness Book of Records.* There he learned of Man's highest achievements. Amazing feats passed before his gaze: fifty-six hard-boiled eggs consumed within the hour; five days non-stop tap-dancing—on one leg only; the comprehensive school that was so progressive that it absorbed all the new ideas before they were ever thought of and so became a museum of new ideas. But, amongst all these wonders, there was one entry which made the learned man very sad.

The Philosopher closes the book and becomes morose. The drum beats sadly as the 1st Minstrel goes to the cart and takes from it a dinner on a plate which he offers to the Philosopher who refuses it

For days he refused to eat. (*He returns the dinner to the cart*) He was unable to sleep. He paced up and down not knowing what to do.

The Philosopher paces morosely and returns to his stool

The entry which had so saddened the philosopher was the one of the ogre which said that he was filled so full of hatred that he could not eat his dinner, even when it was beefburgers and chips. Eventually, the philosopher had an idea.

Drum roll

He knew, because he was so wise, that no-one with sparkling eyes can be full of hatred. So he decided to seek out the ogre and make his eyes sparkle. Stopping only to put a tin of Brasso in his bag, he leapt on to his horse and galloped to the other side of the world, which was also called the Antipodes and caused the postman great confusion.

The Philosopher goes to the cart with the book under his arm. He takes the tin of Brasso and the duffel bag, which he puts over his shoulder, and a hobby horse, which he mounts and "rides" across to R *to the "Antipodes", accompanied by appropriate sounds from the drum*

Eventually, he arrived at the ogre's castle and knocked on the door.

The 4th Minstrel simulates knocking on the drum

Opening the door, the ogre saw the philosopher and was filled with hatred and loathing for him. The philosopher asked the ogre if he might borrow his eyes for he wished to make them sparkle, at which the ogre beat the philosopher over the head with *Ye Guinness Book of Records* which, being a tome of some weight, caused the philosopher to fall down as if dead.

The Ogre and Philosopher act out this scene with the Ogre taking the book from under the Philosopher's arm with which to hit him over the head

Coming to his senses, the philosopher decided to try new methods of making the ogre's eyes sparkle. He went to the local market where he bought a nightingale in a cage.

The Philosopher goes to the cart and takes from it an imaginary nightingale in a cage. He comes downstage C *and speaks to the audience*

Philosopher This——
1st Minstrel He thought.
Philosopher —will make the ogre's eyes sparkle.
1st Minstrel But, when he knocked on the castle door, the ogre seized the cage with the nightingale in it flung it as far as he could into the distance.

The Philosopher and the Ogre mime this scene. The Philosopher runs to the cart

The philosopher ran away in terror and the cage broke releasing the nightingale, which demonstrates the truth of the saying: "It's an ill wind that blows nobody good". The philosopher, determined to make the ogre's eyes sparkle, returned to the market where he purchased a golden harp that played the most beautiful music imaginable.

The Philosopher takes an imaginary harp from the cart to the Ogre's "door"

Once more he knocked upon the castle door. The ogre was furious, seized the golden harp and broke it over the head of the unfortunate philosopher.

The Ogre and Philosopher mime this scene

The philosopher was beginning to develop a headache by now. But he determined to try one more time. He returned to the market where he bought a beautiful mirror in a silver frame.

The Philosopher goes to the cart and takes from it an imaginary mirror which he takes downstage C. *He speaks to the audience*

Philosopher When the ogre sees how ugly all this hatred makes him——
1st Minstrel Thought the philosopher.
Philosopher —he will mend his ways and begin to smile.
1st Minstrel Taking the precaution of wearing a crash helmet on his head, the philosopher made his way once more to the ogre's castle.

The Philosopher goes to the cart, puts a crash helmet on his head, and goes to the Ogre's "door"

He knocked nervously on the door and hid behind the mirror hoping that the ogre would see himself and change his ways.

The Philosopher mimes this

However, when the ogre opened the door, he saw not himself, but another ugly monster full of hatred and loathing. Furious, thinking that this ogre had come to usurp his place in *Ye Guinness Book of Records*, he punched at his rival with all his might.

The Ogre "opens the door" and aims a punch at the imaginary mirror. There are noises, off, of breaking glass and the Philosopher performs a backward somersault. The Ogre sinks to the ground—dead

The ogre's fist hit the mirror with a mighty crash; his wrist was so badly cut that his life blood ran out leaving him dead upon the ground and the philosopher returned home, very glad that he had worn a crash helmet.

The 1st, 3rd and 4th Minstrels move downstage, bow to the audience and exit R *with the handcart*

The 2nd Minstrel rises from the ground, moves downstage and bows to the audience

2nd Minstrel Farewell. I regret that I am unable to continue but there is not a drop of blood left in my body and I am merely a shadow of my former self.

Black-out

The 2nd Minstrel exits and Imagination enters and seats herself on Old King Cole's throne upstage

A spotlight comes up on Imagination

Imagination Thank you, my friends, for releasing me from the foul dungeon of HE. No more shall the Land of Childhood be under the dominion of that evil monster, for behold . . .

Funeral march plays

HE, Sycorax and the Loons enter as a chain-gang

There is a tableau with the chain-gang silhouetted, the spotlight remaining on Imagination. The tabs begin to close slowly as a voice is heard on an off stage microphone

Voice (*off*) Thus it was, O dearly beloved, that the Land of Childhood was rescued from the clutches of HE, Imagination reigned supreme, and civilization survived yet another crisis.

Curtain

FURNITURE AND PROPERTY LIST

Please see Author's Note on page v.

ACT I

SCENE 1

On stage: Log

Off stage: Bucket (**Jack** and **Jill**)

Personal: **Septimus:** wig (worn throughout), mirror
Little Boy Blue: horn (used throughout)

SCENE 2

On stage: Nil

Off stage: Wall **(Stage Management)**

SCENE 3

On stage: Raised throne

SCENE 4

On stage: Nil

SCENE 5

On stage: Transformation chamber
Besom broom
Chest containing spell book
Stool
Cauldron containing stick for stirring

Off stage: Spell ingredients, gag **(Loons)**
Pie **(Loon)**

Personal: **Grimalkin:** copy of *The Witch's Familiar's Weekly*
Lion: torch (practical)
Loons: torches (practical)

ACT II

SCENE 1

On stage: Dais

Personal: **Priest:** card which reads "APPLAUSE"

SCENE 2

On stage: Gaunt tree
Log

Personal: **Loons:** tree branches, rope

SCENE 3

On stage: Nil

SCENE 4

On stage: Transformation chamber
Besom broom
Chest
Stool. *On it:* spell book
Cauldron

Off stage: 2 cages (**Loons**)

SCENE 5

On stage: Nil

SCENE 6

On stage: Raised throne
Handcart. *In it:* Ogre mask, 2 stools, beard, book, dinner on a plate, tin of
  Brasso, duffel bag, hobby horse, crash helmet

Personal: **4th Minstrel:** drum
HE: chains
Loons: chains
Sycorax: chains

LIGHTING PLOT

Practical fitting required: concealed light in cauldron
Various simple interior and exterior settings

ACT I   SCENE 1

To open: Bright early morning sunshine effect

No cues

ACT I   SCENE 2

To open: Exterior effect downstage

No cues

ACT I   SCENE 3

To open: Full interior lighting

No cues

ACT I   SCENE 4

To open: Exterior effect downstage

No cues

ACT I   SCENE 5

To open: General interior lighting

Cue 1	**Sycorax:** "... whilst I stir the mixture." *Start gradual fade to Black-out*	(Page 14)
Cue 2	**Sycorax:** "A cat for the world to see." *Practical flashes on and off, then bring up general interior lighting*	(Page 14)
Cue 3	Loud bang *Black-out*	(Page 15)
Cue 4	**Lion** flashes his fingers *Snap on general interior lighting*	(Page 15)
Cue 5	**Billy Bingo:** "... eyes down and looking." *Start gradual fade to Black-out*	(Page 18)

Cue 6   **All: "—BINGO!"**   (Page 18)
             Practical flashes on and off, then bring up general interior lighting

ACT II SCENE 1

To open: General interior lighting

No cues

ACT II SCENE 2

To open: Sombre, dim woodland effect with spot on tree

Cue 7   **Imagination** lies down   (Page 21)
             Lightning, lighting dims, spot flashes on and off

ACT II SCENE 3

To open: Exterior effect downstage

No cues

ACT II SCENE 4

To open: General interior lighting

No cues

ACT II SCENE 5

To open: Exterior effect downstage

No cues

ACT II SCENE 6

To open: Bright interior lighting

Cue 8   **2nd Minstrel:** "... a shadow of my former self."   (Page 30)
             Black-out

Cue 9   When ready   (Page 30)
             Bring up spot on **Imagination** *upstage*

Cue 10   **HE, Sycorax** and the **Loons** enter as a chain-gang   (Page 31)
             Bring up silhouette effect on chain-gang

EFFECTS PLOT

Please read the notice on page viii regarding the use of copyright material.

ACT I

Cue 1   Before the CURTAIN rises   (Page 1)
Piano nursery-rhyme medley

Cue 2   When CURTAIN rises   (Page 1)
Birdsong, continue throughout scene, and one cuckoo call

Cue 3   **Simple Simon** stretches and yawns   (Page 1)
Cuckoo call

Cue 4   **Mrs Spratt** and the **Old Woman** fight   (Page 3)
"William Tell Overture." Continue

Cue 5   **Septimus** jumps out from behind log   (Page 3)
Cut music

Cue 6   **Septimus** exits   (Page 5)
Piano nursery-rhyme medley for scene change

Cue 7   To open SCENE 3   (Page 6)
Music for dance

Cue 8   **Imagination:** "... find their way there."   (Page 10)
Ominous music to end scene

Cue 9   Lights return to normal   (Page 14)
Loud roar

Cue 10   **Sycorax:** "Come out, nice pussy."   (Page 14)
Loud roar

Cue 11   **Lion** flashes his fingers   (Page 15)
Loud bang

Cue 12   **Lion:** "Unearthly music now descend."   (Page 15)
Music for Dance of Lights

Cue 13   **Lion:** "That's funny—no bang."   (Page 15)
Loud bang

Cue 14   **Sycorax:** "Forward!"   (Page 18)
Chopin's Funeral March

ACT II

Cue 15   When the CURTAIN rises   (Page 19)
Church organ music. Continue

Cue 16   Priest holds up card   (Page 19)
Taped applause, abruptly cut (optional). Church music changes to organ version of "Happy Days Are Here Again"

Cue 17   To open SCENE 2   (Page 20)
Owl hoot

Cue 18   **Imagination** lies down   (Page 21)
Thunder

Cue 19   To open SCENE 6   (Page 25)
Music for **Fiddlers'** *dance*

Cue 20   **Ogre** mimes punching imaginary mirror   (Page 30)
Breaking glass

Cue 21   **Imagination:** "... for behold."   (Page 30)
Chopin's Funeral March

MADE AND PRINTED IN GREAT BRITAIN BY
LATIMER TREND & COMPANY LTD PLYMOUTH

MADE IN ENGLAND

www.ingramcontent.com/pod-product-compliance
Ingram Content Group UK Ltd.
Pitfield, Milton Keynes, MK11 3LW, UK
UKHW021821150726
7214IPUK00017B/260